DIASPORADIC

Winner of the 1997 Marianne Moore Poetry Prize

*The Marianne Moore Poetry Prize
was established in 1991 by Helicon Nine Editions,
and is awarded annually to a previously unpublished
manuscript chosen by a distinguished writer
through an open nationwide competition.*

The judge for 1997 was Molly Peacock.

DIASPORADIC

poems

PATTY SEYBURN

Winner of the
1997 Marianne Moore Poetry Prize

Foreword by Molly Peacock

HELICON NINE EDITIONS
KANSAS CITY, MISSOURI

Grateful acknowledgment is made to the editors of the following magazines
in which these poems first appeared, sometimes in slightly different versions:
ACM (Another Chicago Magazine), The Bellingham Review, The Beloit Poetry
Journal, The Cimarron Review, Connecticut Review, The Formalist, Hubbub,
New England Review, The Paris Review, Western Humanities Review, Press,
Best of Writers at Work, 1995

Cover and book design: Tim Barnhart
Cover photograph: *Ambassador Bridge*, Burton Historical
Collection, Detroit Public Library

Helicon Nine Editions is funded in part by the National Endowment
for the Arts, a federal agency, and by the Kansas Arts Commission
and the Missouri Arts Council, state agencies.

Library of Congress Cataloging -in-Publication Data

Seyburn, Patty, 1962-
    Diasporadic : poems / Patty Seyburn. -- 1st ed.
      p.   cm.
    ISBN 1-884235-26-3 : (on acid-free paper)
    I. Title.
PS3569.E88637D5   1998
811'.54--dc21   98-30774
                                                                         CIP

First Edition

Printed in the United States of America.
Helicon Nine Editions

CONTENTS

III.

INTRODUCTION

What distinguishes Patty Seyburn's first volume of poetry, *Diasporadic*, is her magic habit of managing disparate but simultaneous perspectives. Almost yoga-like, she seems able to train her focus at once on big subjects and small details, as if she had a different capacity for perspective than the rest of us. This allows the whole range of human emotions into her poetry, not just the noble ones. Thus, she can take on talking to God about issues of existence while poking the deity with tiny questions. "Why peppermint *and* spearmint?" she pouts. Because of her capacious perspective, her poetry has a saving humor even as it tackles the events of love and death. One of the book's most startling images is that of the floating caskets of the Jews washed out of their cemetery in the collection's title poem. "Oh, we're wandering again," Patty Seyburn blurts out, rescuing catastrophe with the life-raft of a pun.

Long lines, short lines, free verse, formal verse, lyrics, and narratives—she ranges comfortably in wide prosodic territory, unconfined by neither a narrow vista nor a narrowness of technique, allowing us as readers to range widely, too, investigating her subjects and ideas and witnessing her interests and history. Seyburn takes her time when she mulls things over, indulging in her musing. She is willing to risk our impatience because such slowness is essential to the well-lived life. And the well-lived life, according to Seyburn, is the one vulnerable to the sudden recognition of emotion, as she demonstrates so ably in the moving poem, "The Follow," in which a man with two prosthetic legs attempts to waltz with his wife. The idea of such a poem could lead to disaster in less capable hands.

What is new about these poems is their unsureness, the un-authority of this author as she makes her way. Her poems are created from an alluring willingness not to know all the answers, and thus to be available to interpret the world for us flexibly, in all it's excitement and mystification. "If you had asked me, *What can I do?* I might have asked you / to balance my checkbook...," she ventures in "Any Day

Now," illuminating the vastness of mourning with the particularity of the daily details that no one can master in the face of loss. The speaker comforts herself—and charms us—by allowing herself to be overwhelmed.

Seyburn's poems range through thousands of years of history. From Ruth and Naomi to Yoko Ono, from Pythagoras to the route of a city bus, this is a poet who leaves in the nubs as she weaves a very contemporary woman's fabric, calling upon heritage and pop culture to create the landscape where she will set her loves and losses, connecting to others as she reconnects with her identity as a Jew.

Haven't we met before? I ask myself all during my reading and re-reading of the anonymously submitted *Diasporadic*. It turned out that Patty Seyburn and I had met, in fact. When her name was revealed, I realized that I had read her early work in the Barnard College Writers on Writing Program, and kept on for a bit afterward. We lost touch then, though in the larger universe we seem to have remained connected. Now it is a personal delight to introduce this strong and complex first book, recipient of the 1997 Marianne Moore Poetry Prize.

—Molly Peacock
Judge

I.

How strange it seems! These Hebrews in their graves,
    Close by the street of this fair seaport town,
Silent beside the never-silent waves,
    At rest in all this moving up and down!
                —Henry Wadsworth Longfellow

Diasporadic

When I saw the Jews floating, I knew
it was time to pack up, when the water
struck their oak boxes, the small stones
placed atop their graves in memory
scattering, the great slabs engraved
like charms on a bracelet swept
downstream as though rocks were
driftwood, rocks were feathers—
in our game, paper bested rocks
which crippled scissors, anyway—
and I put on my tall rubber boots,
zipped my duffle that could be lifted
high as a child overhead and made
my way toward the flume—now dry,
water rising on both sides, resembling
the Red Sea's cinematic parting, smudged
extras trudging a swath of sand, pretending
that God split the sea for them clean
as a perfect center part in wet hair,
while De Mille's technicians shot jello
at high-speed. I saw Jews' caskets freed
from cemetery Beth Yeshurun meandering
downtown, bumping into names, dates
and epitaphs, a few trees, I thought
oh, we're wandering, again. I suppose
there's no point in following the dead:
on present course, they'll run the bayous
with no regard for rapids and whitewater
chutes, careen into the Gulf, ocean-bound—
the Atlantic, the one they crossed long ago,
the Old Country newly inviting. I can't go
with them, though I was a fine swimmer
once, the one assigned the race's last leg,

who could make up time lost with long
strokes, cupped hands, strong kick, when I
turned my head for breaths I saw the others
fall behind. My distant family, my distant
lover, called for me to leave weeks ago—but
who knew that the heavens were so full?
that cumulonimbus could store centuries
of rain? No ark this time, no dove nor
olive branch, only the dry land we've made,
this slow sluice—do you see the floating Jews'
nomadic names and bodies propelled
by the waters—*now where are they going?*

Turret

Outside, the dark flags wrap and unwrap
the poles, flick them like steam-breathing
children cracking the whip on the ice rink.

I remember the end of an S-curve, waiting
to fly—did I steal that memory from Hans Brinker?
Reading him made me want to be Dutch,

the Bobsey Twins offered a mirroring brother,
those prairie books caused my craving for creamed
potatoes and peas, but my mom said, *We're Jews,*

we don't eat like that. We lived in a house built
of dark-red brick, three stories, the main stairwell
curled to a landing half-way down, and split—

choose your end, den or foyer. Once I rolled down,
head tucked, arms hugging my knees, taking
the curve—wait, I think that I made that up.

Winds there pressed up and out of the lake—
they'd flatten me onto frigid brick until my back
was brick—but I was elastic, a cartoon character,

nothing to fear but mirth. Here, flags gauge
the wind-god's ire or boredom—I hear him
pacing invisible tunnels, hissing in loneliness,

while I am fortressed, framed in my window sash.
If cars slowed on that fast road that moats my home,
they'd see me in states of undress that span

the day's transit to dark, then my silhouette—
but they don't. With my fingers, I comb through my
bottomless hair, hum a ballad, offering someone

their chance at a damsel distressed. Still, no
takers. And my memories, built on story, fade
fast into story, these fictions once mine now

keeping me in: I fear that I'm fiction. The window
gives back my bed, my shelf—history, diary—
a candle, my body. Each day I think *maybe today*

and wait for the flags that guard me, chide me—
come out, they say, *don't come out*—to tire of
beckoning, tire of shaking their fists.

lower case

I caught a glimpse of god inside
the pecan tree out back. It's hard
to tell, but you get used to the signs.
Leave that tree alone, I said.
He shook a low branch.
An unripe pecan fell.
Now look what you've done, I said.
Now you've done it. He shrugged.

This has been going on for awhile.
Yesterday I found him under the divan.
I chided him: *You can't hide forever.*
Watch me, he said.
I told him, *I don't like you
looking at my feet.* No answer.
I'm going to mop. With ammonia.
Then I did.

At first, I had a few questions.
The big ones. And smaller ones:
Why peppermint *and* spearmint?
Earlobes? Lichen? Killer bees?

He spent last week sitting
on our porch, on the wooden swing
with the rusty chain. Smoking.
I know, I know, he said. *Just one.*
Fine, I said. *Kill yourself. Who would know?*
He snubbed it out and tossed
the butt into a clump of brambles
with a thousand other butts.

Sometimes he disappears
for days, for weeks. I know enough

not to scold or praise his return.
I let myself say: *you could call.*

I say: *Why don't you make yourself
useful?* He says: *I have no skills.
I flunked the temp typing test.
Computers confuse me.
And filing—well, filing
I shouldn't have to do.*
I tell him: *be a paper clip. A staple.
People always run out.*

He's a whiz, however, at the *New York Times*
crossword. He knows that Erse
is Gaelic, the length of the Nile, and all
the synonyms for zenith.
And he doesn't ask much:
the odd, hardboiled egg;
a nice piece of whitefish, boned;
a tomato on the cusp of ripeness.

You like that? I ask. He nods
approval, chews slowly, quietly,
not wanting to intrude. At times,
I hardly know he's there.

Inversion

The tram's steel fingers clutch the plait of wires,
and the steel box slides down the mountain,

leveling off three times, three dips and glides.
A woman screams her pleasure. A baby grips

her father's sleeve in her fist, eyes blooming
to welcome more light. And the ark of the air

rocks, the way Noah's boat, carrying chosen pairs
would have yawed enough to remind them

of what they'd been told to pack: awe and luck.
A desert city flicks on its lights. A floor of stars,

heaven's terrain. The woman's thoughts are louder
than the grace note, downbeat of her heart. She wonders,

as of a dream so alive that it begs to switch places
with the real, which direction they are going.

The Follow

Suppose that his mother taught him to dance

that she ordered her youngest son into the living room,
humming Strauss. *An Austrian*, she shrugged, *they're not so bad*.

that she showed him where to place his hands,
applying only the pressure of the wind's palm
on the laurel's slim waist, and she thought, *I am a laurel*
and laughed, ten children plumbed from her womb.

that she counted: one-two-three, one-two-three, speaking
in rhythm so he would hear nothing but one-two-three
while he relied on his will to please and a steady grip
to learn the shift of weight and momentum.

that she proceeded to lead, step forward so he would
step back, step left, adding the angle until they were
circling his infinite possibilities, and the crooked floor
creaked, unwilling to buoy joy unattached to occasion.

that she said: a gesture. a glance. slight pressure. *Use what you have*.

Suppose, a lifetime later, he wanted to dance with his wife,
her yellow tulle dress pale as a lemon's inside, and he leaned
on two crutches, shifting the weight from two plastic legs
that replaced his two bloodless legs, which had died.

that he willed each fake leg into its role, repeatedly,
drafting the placement and size of a step, measuring effort
in terms of result, ghost pain in each extension, and he walked,
each step its own aching arc, to the edge of the parquet floor.

that he tried to remember the waltz, then laughed and thought,
I am no laurel—one hand on a crutch, the other lightly alit
on my mother's pastel back as she swayed, and he hummed,
luring the triplets home to his body, hoping for instinct.

Suppose that his legs obeyed.

Any Day Now

If you had asked me, *What can I do?* I might have asked you
to balance my checkbook, or handed you a hamper of dirty
whites, your pleasant face surprised but your hands open,
taking it—or I might have said, stay here and answer

the phone when it rings at odd times, stay and sleep with me—
you know what I mean. You could fix my air conditioner,
which rumbles, or take that note of pity from my mother's
voice. "I worry," she says, "because you don't have anyone."

I try to conjure up my father's ghost—that should not be so
hard, so soon after, he is probably still lingering, wondering
how to fill his time now that the full-time job of suffering
is over. I watch lightning strobe against the tile floor

and friends call to tell me they love me and that sounds
lovely but solves nothing, speaks to nothing and invites
even more of it. Twisted candle after twisted candle burns
down, blue and white two-wicked candles of mourning.

People mill through the apartment now my mother's,
the bedroom door closed, hiding props: wheelchair,
bedpan and syringe, pill and prosthesis. I look like
my father but not near the end, his cheeks' oval bloom

cut to angles; then I knew he was old. The cold-cut trays
too heavy to pass, we've got a nice spread and I try to clear
plates but the well-intended take them, all that's left for
me to do is bury my nails in my palms, dent moons, blood

blisters. I talk as though the sounds I make make any
sense at all. I found him in a dream, I can't remember
what he said or even his voice but he was walking
with no walker—the picture he'd have chosen,

not the later one of weakness and need—a brief interval,
but order can't be ignored. We are victims of sequence.

The exigent now compresses the width and breadth
of before, folds the flat square into a cube that takes up

less room on the urgent surface, like skin that rents
then collects itself to scar. And yet we can "vanish"
the recent the way magicians shorthand their rabbits.
The phone call that taught me to fear an early ring

could be this morning or a date long since mourned.
Face it, time is a mess, all lurches and jars, distended.
Who would have thought that the world would go on
this long without him? Even now, I think it will end.

Mourning

Untouched by grief, you want to know its heft,
assay it in your palm's mimetic bowl
the way Egyptians sought to weigh the soul,
so weighed the body once the soul had left.
They found their scales defective, imprecise;
unable to detect, much less discern.
So would your senses, at both bow and stern
of reason, realize themselves a vise.

But I can give you what it is you crave:
here is a moment bursting with despair
that you may carry with you like spare change—
collected daily, can't be spent or saved,
worth little—but the coins are somehow rare,
that nonetheless, you would *would not* exchange.

Claims

        I know a woman whose husband set himself on fire

and did not die soon enough. Did he think he deserved
the full complement of pain, or to persuade his family
that he hated not them, but life in all its trappings—
        flesh, decor, maintenance?

No, she says. He was miserable, crazy. She pieces together
his words, singed clues—those her mind forgives her,
released to her sanity's charge, as though one can assemble
        a puzzle of ash,

stray sparks of grief and anger housed in her eye. She curses
all the abstractions he lauded—beauty, absolution, purity—
onerous hopes that hinged on escape, his act of ownership:
        this body is mine.

        I know a man who stood atop his home to defend

his few possessions from flame's ambition, hosing down
roof and walls to create a protective sheath of water.
And his work begot a miracle: fire snapped in his direction,
        but declared him and his unworthy.

Around him, scorched remains, vacant as the plains of Ararat
after the Great Flood cleaned house by destruction, demanding:
Start over. And so when the Lord surveyed the rise and raze
        of his ever-revising domain,

He slipped the gift of forgetting into the human gut, so man
could wake without fear of chaos fleeing and reversing
its course, so woman's remorse (memory of the corporeal pyre,
        its strange grandeur) would wane.

        They say the Torah was written in black fire on white fire.

Stone Notes

The tour guide said, consider the nature of age
and multiply that by a number you can't fathom—
the prime, the irrational, the lounging eight of infinity.

> *Go away, says the stone. I'm shut tight.*

I wedded the two abstractions, and wondered how many
the brain could hold, like a hand that splays into
a question's gesture, exposing the palm's shallow bowl,
the fingers' distinctions, then closing into a fist.

> IF THOU MAKE ME AN ALTAR,
> THOU SHALT NOT BUILD IT OF HEWN STONE,
> FOR IF THOU LIFT UP THY TOOL UPON IT,
> THOU SHALT PROFANE IT.

My father's doctor held up his fist to model the heart.
When he unfurled it, we saw the map of auguring lines,
and the obligations of surface: protect, prevent, provide.

> *My whole surface is turned toward you,*
> *all my insides turned away*

Contemplation, the tour guide said, would behoove us,
these slabs a locus of ritual, heal stone ushering light
down an avenue into the heart of the sacrosanct circle.

> ASSEMBLE THE CONGREGATION, AND SPEAK YE
> UNTO THE ROCK BEFORE THEIR EYES.

And though I did my best to comply, all I could see
was my mother's face in the camera's automatic eye,
exposing her question: what stops the heart?
I framed her gaze in ruins, huge bluestones that teams
of worshippers scraped across Salisbury's undulant plain.

> *You may get to know me,*

but you'll never know me through.

Did death please this god of hyperbole, lord of myopia
issuing orders in bolt and flash for scale and simplicity?
Did he mean these incomplete arcs, sarsens and lintels
pulleyed into place, to outlive his chain of command?

> AND HE GAVE UNTO MOSES
> TWO TABLES OF TESTIMONY,
> TABLES OF STONE, WRITTEN
> WITH THE FINGER OF GOD.

I think of a game contained in a child's witless hands:
rock paper scissors. By instinct, she decides:
destruct, dissemble, divide.

> *You shall not enter, says the stone.*
> *You lack the sense of taking part.*

I think of creatures made of stone,
their temples celebrations of self,
each idol a cousin once removed.

> NEITHER SHALL YE PLACE
> ANY FIGURED STONE IN YOUR HAND,
> TO BOW DOWN UNTO IT.

Perhaps they've exhausted their mineral sources,
and in our hedged and rowed, fenced-in conventions
of the dead, they'll find utility, even salvation.

> *No other sense can make up*
> *for your missing sense of taking part.*

They'll use my father's marker as a hand

> AND UNDER HIS FEET...A PAVED WORK OF SAPPHIRE STONE

And out of that his printing will flow

Just ask the leaf, it will tell you the same.

the color of granite, of lead.

TAKE TWO ONYX, AND GRAVE ON THEM
THE NAMES OF THE CHILDREN OF ISRAEL.

And out of that a note
that they don't know where to send,
saying, thank you, thank you,
you poor dead gods.

———————

Italics from "Conversation with a Stone" by Wislawa Szymborska

California

The stones of a singing beach
are thrown atop each other.
When the tide remits,
stones sing as the water sifts
through, reshifting the layers
like when I climb over then under
you who sleep, lightly snoring.
If I were the daymoon, showing its face
with the sky still hysterically blue,
I'd have the grace to look
guilty, an icon of excess light:
we have enough, can't you see?
As for the birds
who trill and prattle by night,
I forgive them their obdurate tunes:
they wake us
so I can revel in your fairness.

Good Water

For C.V.

When the fires found their way up over the Laguna hills
soon to meet the nothingness left by good-guy fires,
backfires officially set to deprive the wild ones

of bounty, to starve them of fodder, we moved in closer
to watch, eye level to hell, a place where destruction
is so beautiful, you can't help staring. Told that rage

must exhaust itself, that flailing water wouldn't help
until the fire stopped to breath, we sat on our heels
outside our frangible houses and saw what burns,

which is almost everything natural, as is the burning
itself. And we knew we were faster than the fires,
that some things that hurt us are slow, or seem slow,

or if truly fast, envelop the time before and after,
claiming their turf the way death dog-ears its place.
Where the fire began has long been abandoned,

though we're not sure where that is—the sun always
first to be questioned when some flame gets loose,
as if every fire was borne of a magnifying glass

and we spend our time trying to impress our symbol
on a dead leaf that ends up a smolder, or wanting
to prove that with a lone prop, we could survive

a cold night in the wilderness, though nights
are no longer cold that way, the coolness
one of indifference: Old God tired of pacts,

New One of healing, and now the sky bleeds
with dogs, bugs, warriors, ladles and ladders flung
by Olympians. But you and I can outrun the hour,

the flame's detour around the charred hills, away
from the numbing sea that would shock your limbs
into forgetting how to save themselves, erasing

memory and its pain, pain and its memory: help
we do not need. Our footprints indent the grass.
We watch. Then run. Why not? While we are fast.

Night Geometry

I watch you fall asleep—the spiral down? ascent?
to the lot of unused brain. I think the journey
lateral—a dance beginning in the hips, a side-stepped
punch, a pass in any sport, by foot or hand,
to redirect the play. No ground is lost or gained.
We love to credit the surreal with real motives,
wrest the clocks and teeth from dreams, lodge them
in a conscious place so that they don't escape,
bend straight-laced steel into a liberating shape.

The Tower of London stamps its image on your lobe,
backdrop for your ancestor's heroic stand—a Scot
against the Brits, the last to lose his head to treason
and the guillotine. His face yours, he waves with death's
insouciance. The blade speeds down (direction) up (in speed)
to greet his neck. You have an urge to know the rate
(velocity): with time and distance you could calculate
but now the head has cut and spun. You weep.
You cringe and grimace in the clutch of sleep.

I dream a game, of trying to break through
a children's enfilade. The other team calls out
for me to infiltrate their line, their hands held fast.
They try to separate my flimsy hands from...yours?
Why are you here? They break our grip. We lose.
You're gone. I want to raze the lines. I want to
even up the score. Instead, I wake and fit along
your curve. We form one line. Our bodies hum.
One running for, the other running from.

Left as I am now

Sometimes I catch myself on a city bus, opening
        my mouth slightly to fit my lips
with your slightly open mouth, one of us askew—we know

by instinct who goes right or left, though I suspect it changes
        each kiss—were I more sensitive
to detail, I'd notice how each of us yaws, and were we

too predictable, suggest that we switch—I would hate
        to bore you by always tilting left
as I am now. A red-haired man stares at my mouth, the way

my eyes fall to your mouth and stay there as I near the mark—
        he models his lips after mine
like a child whose lips part as the spoon approaches, mimicking

the feeder, and a balding punk girl sneers at me. I'm thinking
        of that light-board sign with scrolling
words that rose over I-405, care of Don Kott's Used Cars,

proclaiming, "IN A LOVER'S EYES, POCKMARKS R DIMPLES"
        (no room for the full "are," predicate
dispensable, get in and out quickly as you can);

soon block letters mutated into "FLOOD SALE!" then into
        "VALENTINE'S DAY DEALS ON THUNDERBIRDS"—
oracular, the last word owning its own line—if the driver

remembers nothing else, he'll remember, "Thunderbirds" or
        "dimples," the highway harbinger
presaging desire—I'd like the last word, I'd like you

to think of my pockmarks as dimples, to give me an active
        verb. Punk girl, newly clairvoyant,
speaks out, leaning in like a confidante, *Where is he?*

as if I could tell her, and redhead chimes in, their voices
          both rise in the middle, on the "is,"
and all the slumped denizens, waiting for a sign, straighten up,

join in, their voices are dominos falling, following
          the other's lead, *Where is he?*
The bus surges forward, contrapuntal, numbered streets count

down until I think that this chorus of absence will burst
          my head open—see how easy
it is to rile up a crowd, how much power you have.

Complaint to the Management

Unsure of where I stand on loneliness,
I shut the shed-doors on a petulant wind,
coax the lock through the chain's loops,
my car at home amidst misfit theater props,
old coolers, ownerless tools, and know
I won't be taking the I-10 West, looping
San Antonio and Phoenix to see you in
your California town, a set table of land
near the ocean's lip. Not this night,
my red Ford relieved to escape another
1,600 miles, though I am starting to miss
the soup-to-nuts sky of west Texas
sashaying across my windshield. It's only
tourist terrain for me, not an expanse
I live with daily, not the gap between
your voice's curves and your head resting
in my ribcage, a bed of thinly covered bones,
though I sleep better when my car's tank
is full, and a jug of water freights the backseat.
The idea of compulsion, if not compulsion
itself, propels me through days whose hours
move like languorous limbs underwater.
I'd like to file a complaint: too much
compromise, the air is heavy with it, and
too few snacks in the bar. The ironic cat,
purple in its blackness, treads on my heels,
though he's just leaped to the outside world
via my torn screen, and I am half-relieved,
half-bitter that no one's plans or hopes
hinge on my arrival. He precedes underfoot,
refusing to be the last one in—or worse,
to be caught waiting, as I'm found wanting
to find somewhere want doesn't live.

When

By day, want quiet
because you can't have it:
the street basks in traffic's attention,
neighbors practice the emphatic
slamming of doors, breeze invites
the murmur of leaves' detritus.
You think, *they're conspiring*
but know that's not true. There's no
intention. You shouldn't be so
worried about others.

By night, want noise
because you can't have it:
wind's machinations are so subtle
you fear you've made them up.
And anyway, they're not loud enough.
You need dogs' ears, tuned
to a frequency that doesn't
allow or condone sounds' escape,
interrogating notes and timbres
like the cop who loves his work

which is why, in winter,
when your half of the earth
is partial to darkness, you need
the ocean, its serial slap on sand
that for all its submitting
to tides and tows, is intransigent.
That's a good model for you.
You need to be tougher—
when the pleasures of solitude ebb,
to pull your feet from the suck.

Nantasket Beach, Briefly

For a moment, I saw myself swathed in a future
       I didn't even realize I wanted: a beach town hushed
with old money, Victorians tiered as cakes
       (complete with pedestaled plastic bride and groom)
sliced deep into hillsides, Adirondack chairs sprawled
       on wrap-around porches for watching the sea
as good Easterners will.

Surprised at my Cabot and Lowell aspirations,
       I followed you room to room and planned
where everyone would sleep when this place was ours,
       when we dug our heels into the soil beneath
your family tree, your name carved into concentrics,
       each ring. I never knew I wanted a history
other than that of my own name

changed at the Canadian border, contracted
       by syllable and consonant to comfort the New World's ear.
My family's remote rich branch talked like you,
       recondite R's, a new country brogue I thought meant
Irish, Catholic, Kennedy—but mine were glamorous
       Jewish girls wed to Boston's fast Jewish boys—
mafia, said gossip,

so I pictured threats in fedoras, coded cognomens
       that worked a double-shift, "Lou the Butcher"
and adopted the story of a man whose specialty
       was slamming thumbs in doors of Lincoln towncars.
They summered in Jackie O shades
       (I had never known a season turned verb)
on their island, offered

off-the-shoulder invitations, urging my parents,
       Send her here so the civilized seaboard would purge me

of midwestern tone, a singsong of minimal
        musical merit. Sent? I came on my own
and found no new voice, only an old one,
        the chorus of a singing beach shuffling its stones,
farther out the cries

of fear and curiosity, coupled. To your nephew I sang
        a minor-key lullaby; and in its diminished chords
he recognized his cue to sleep. Weepy from the slap
        of Atlantic air, the storm of aunts and uncles come
to praise him, the child lay down his head in my neck's cove
        and cloaked his face in my hair. Pleasure swam
across your mouth—

I saw it—for a second he was ours. The house, ours.
        Chairs, ours. Contentment—ours, too—all that was hard
eased in a fit of possession. I envisioned us
        on your island, steeped in layers of stories,
spectral wives' journals that I would be
        next to embellish...*At night I pace*
the Widow's Walk...

(she sees lights tiny as a pinhead, sailing
        arcs, ghost ships tacking an enigmatic sea)
I sing to distract myself (the ocean sighs at women
        casting words into water) *I sing in case they're lost*
(petition and moan like line and lure
        knotted in kelp, stranded on the berm)
At night I pace.

Then, what was ours disappeared.
        The flare of the possible fled from your face
to a room I'll never find, let alone inhabit.
        There will be no record of the history
I glimpsed, the drape of my voice, my name's
        revision. My notes join hers. I don't expect *I don't*
expect him to return.

Spreading the Word

i. Marie De L'Incarnation, 1654

"The apostolic fire burned in her heart,"
son Claude declared, while cleansing her prose
of its *rudesse*—he'd graciously impart
a note of moderation, strip the rose
of scent. Why risk offending *politesse*
with talk of "inner union," "ravishment,"
her mother's mortal hatred of her flesh?
The widow's chastity her ornament.

She sailed to Canada to teach the name
of Christ—"C'est mon moi"—"He is my me"—
to clear the path that led away from shame.
Those she called *filles sauvages* called her *sainte fille*.
Claude praised the "inner sweetness" of her word;
her passion, though edited, endured.

ii. Maria Sybilla Merian, 1683

Her second volume opened with the bees,
their watercolor/copperplate and text—
their schizophrenic hues, the way they tease
reluctant nectar from the bloom with dextrous
tongues, their syncopated whirr of life,
their constancy—devotion to the world
that God assigned: the confines of the hive.
No fevered bloom to plunder, workers swirled
around her hands. *They never leave,* she thought.
She had a love of leaving that her spouse
did not condone, and with her daughter bought
two berths to Surinam, to set up house.
She lauded bees' existence, called them "pure."
Adept, they spend their lives eluding her.

iii. Glikl bas Judas Leib, 1689

Betrothed to Hayim Hamel at age twelve,
she steeped her life in his until his death
and in her grief's excess, began to tell
herself a story, trying to accept
the sorrows that would come for tea and stay,
the comfort of the *tkhines* prayers she read,
the Messianic promises delayed,
her loss, her *koved*—love and honor—dead.

She took a pen, and wrote, and soon declared
the first of seven volumes, done: a stew
of narrative, advice, confession, prayer,
the complicated exile of the Jew.
She left the "other nations" to their din.
She thought, *I've barely time for my own sin.*

Push Back, the Shore

When I stretch, it must be blood I hear
veering through my ventricles and veins,
an ornate city, though I share the island's
disposition, and feel distinctly peninsular,
an offshoot, connected by way of a gesture:
two lanes, an eyelash's width on a map.
I live on a finger, a spit of land singularly
vertical, bounded by ocean and bay,
horizon and port. When I want to imagine,
I peer West to the blue plain beveled
by the eye's sway; sails, jetties and piers,
silhouettes lauding the need to interrupt
the sea's stab at endlessness. I turn East
to the boats, an enfilade tied in Gordian
slip knots, scoured clean so their monikers—
Nevertheless, Sweet Sofia, Freudian Sloop—
stand out like intaglios, inscribing identities
on memory's lobe against Lethe's wish,
as they slide from sight into a congress
of vessels that circle en route to erasure.
Bracketed, nightly I hear my own blood
wandering in search, in winter, when
the air is anonymous. Bullying waves
from the ocean's barrel chest push back
the indecisive shore, pummel and tow
each shell, each tendril of kelp, partial
castles and moats—and still, the shore repels
the wave, and my own current calms.
The pleasure boats begin to stir, loosen
their ropes' dumb allegiance to the dock;
unable to break the grip, they beckon me
to free them with familiar pleas and lies,
those we believed when fear was more

phantom than knowledge of the finite.
I won't hurt you, says one of the boats.
Don't be scared...Don't you want to know
what's out there? It says: *I'll bring you back.*

II.
SORORITY

Orpah, Revising

Naomi said, *Go home girls, I'm cursed,*

and we clutched, cried *No! No!*
the proper length of time. Then
Ruth and I went—or so I thought—
our families' grasping hands eager
to marry us off again, used goods.
We had grown close while the men
gleaned and politicked, dealt chance
games, made predictions, shared
versions of God. Slouching home coiled
to half their height, eyes and fingers
stained with prayer, still mumbling.
Numbly remote, even undressed.

Then again…departure wasn't all that glib—
the one mistake so vast it undid
every previous gesture, my husband's
rakish eyes, the camaraderie of sisters.
There are few wrongs we recognize
as we perform them—not that they
send up a flare. Naomi wailing,
Call me Marah! The Almighty hath
afflicted me! Who could blame
her tongue for bitterness? Husband
and two sons—our men—dead, leaving us
three women to the chapped palms

of charity, *tzedakah*, Naomi says
and we repeat the hard syllabics,
a premise I learn and unlearn
from every town fool we meet,
when we give what we don't have.
No more sons for you girls, she moans,

and none for me—as if we could wait
twenty years, wombs desiccating
each day the sun stuns the wheat
and sheaves release random strands,
afterthoughts on which the poor
feed, meager handfuls of harvest.

Twice Naomi tried to send us home
and we refused—where is home,
after all, once you marry? With
the strident father, stern brother
in their circumscribed rooms?
On her third round of pleas, I took
the cue. I'm not the type to dwell.
I told myself: *alone, she'll merit pity
if not mercy.* Ruth agreed—or so
I thought. We kissed Naomi's creased
hands and face. Did I taste a twinge
of guilt? Hear a note of futurity,

a chord from David's lyre,
echo of Solomon's refrain? No,
I had no seer's glimpse. We left (or so
I thought) and next I'm hearing
rumor of my sister-in-law's "high style,"
diction of holy men, lawyers,
self-declared prophets on a binge.
Entreat me not to leave thee.
Ruthie, who'd have known?
Such a flare for iambs and petition.
Whither thou goest, I will go...
Parallel structure? Repetition?

Ah well, it's the nondescript
that show you up, I'm told.
I'm not the jealous type; she saw
a niche and molded herself to it.

No nobility in chances missed.
Still, it's demeaning. After one mention,
I'm scrubbed from the scrolls,
her simple name scrawled across
scripture, Midrash, Mishnah,
lines quoted, requited, among
the purest ever uttered
(and from a Moabite's mouth!)

a testament to loyalty…stubbornness,
I say. Still, her compromise is not
one I'd choose—electing to become
a Jew—of all the gods to opt for,
why Him? Nothing to look at.
Always mad. Spate of laws leaving
little time leftover to enjoy the cool
"threshing floor." I tell and retell
myself this rationale for leaving,
for error, fame's window carved
in its wake—but I thought my decision
the long shot (since when does adventure

come to *you?*) and (a gambler at heart)
I relied on risk's habit of begetting reward.
How could I tell that risk was disguised
as an old, depressed woman, as inertia
lodged in a lovesick girl, obeying
Naomi's meted details: *graze and follow,
uncover his feet, give yourself over
to Him, to Boaz, and history* all
in one act, one night (rumor has it
Boaz died the next) which was just
enough: *And Boaz begot Obed; and Obed
begot Jesse, and Jesse begot David.*

And David slew Goliath, who some
claim was my progeny, and I won't

dignify that story with denial,
though it earns me a mention
in the commentaries, implying
that I, too, earned my place, my
lesson: Never be the first to leave?
Too flip. Always reconsider? Consider
the pillar of salt remaining, indecision
punished down to particle. I gave
my husband but refused to give myself,
joining the ranks of dispensable figures

who function as props in the capable
heroine's hands. History needs no
facts, only rumors—then it worries
the details until you are greater
than any one voice, vaster than a page
or smaller than a phoneme,
dispersed as the desert into which
my story and I disappeared.
Don't Jews echo Ruth's recital
each spring? Doesn't Cain's mark
still haunt some skins? Luck sticks
to a few, strands others, and coolly

dismisses the rest to oblivion.

Jephthah's Daughter Signs Her Name

And Jephthah vowed unto the Lord: 'If Thou wilt indeed deliver
the children of Ammon into my hand, then it shall be, that whatsoever
cometh forth of the doors of my house to meet me, when I return
shall be the Lord's, and I will offer it up for a burnt offering.'

Judges 11

That would be me—my reward for faith in the filial.
        Never again
will I run to meet anyone: no lover, friend, not the girl
        who tipped my nails in coral glaze,
no rebbe or prophet could make me step a foot
        beyond these walls.
Why would I?

The last time I heard my father's steps, his men's
        victorious huzzas,
I flung open the door (with histrionic flare), ran to greet him
        with timbrels and dances—
and his face fell: "Alas, daughter, you have brought me low!
        I have uttered a vow
that I cannot retract!"

Why do men make such covenants, rules they cannot break
        on penalty
of God's unwieldy wrath? His capricious take on mercy
        turns rain to tempest,
staff to serpent, whale to vessel. Who can predict?
        One day you're wheat,
the next, chaff;

today manna, tomorrow, unleavened bread, the taste and texture
        of necessity:
sun-spackled dough with no penchant for pleasure,

only the dry fact
of sustenance. All I have: this mountain shack.
        Locked-in now
of my own accord.

"Fear of the marketplace" I hear the rebbe tell curious tourists.
        If the story had its way,
I should have gone nobly to the mountains, bemoaning
                my virginity
for two months before submitting to my father's
        oath and sword.
I said: *you have mistaken Him*

for neighboring gods: Baal, Astarte, Chemosh. Have you forgotten
        the angel sent to halt
Abraham's piloted hand when Isaac lay on the altar? But my father,
                born of a whore,
with a mind that aligns men for battle, "vowed a vow"—
        "shook on it"—
I promised. I promised.

Instead, I retreated—fled—to anonymity: reclusive,
        redactive.
I've gained no knowledge in exile, found no
                "good-faith clauses"
on which to build my case. And the mountain has
        no secrets for a virgin
that the town can't answer in chorus.

I've heard a daughter called a "vain treasure,"
        lest she be seduced:
a harlot, unmarried, barren...a witch! I query:
                what kind of treasurer
is a father who gives away his daughter, wedding her fate
        not to another man's fortune,
but to the Angel of Death?

I would deprive that scythe, annul that nuptial
       ketubah contract.
I've survived; to what end? I can't leave, won't leave
          this house.
Outside lies death—thank you, I'll stay in, confined
       by one who gave "his word."
What good is one word

without another? My father died limb by limb, scattered
       throughout Gilead,
as though no single place could bear his shame.
          Already older than he, I'll die
uncut, the details of my death stooped beneath
       the stately serif of the Judges' text,
vague, implying blood spilled.

After all, my father made me—and grieving, would have
       slain me—
as though *he* were the injured one, and I were not
       the ram caught by the horns
in a thicket, bound for slaughter. What the hand can do!
       Nineteen bones in choral
worship, capable of burying

meaning beneath spaces, a knife in a waiting child,
       a father in the ground
he gained and sullied. Assuming his legacy
       for cutting a deal, the art of base
negotiation, I'll draw up my contract:
       no loopholes, caveats,
minutiae, conditions,

claims or stipulations to complicate this case
       of identity not mistaken,
but one never given, that would have been taken.
       Like the women I was raised to become,

my home is my world. As well,
       my body is mine. Show me the dotted line
(I've practiced my signature)

and I'll resign myself to these spare rooms,
       and speak no more
of words' hidden coves. I'll make a pact,
       and send the original to Him
whose name we don't know
       how to say—can't say—won't say—from one
who has no name to utter.

Beruryah, Deciding

2nd Century, C.E.

I.

Here is a chair, here is a rope with a looped end coiled
as though to hook an answer to some midrashic melee

concerning the value—not in coin or possession—of life,
once arrogance (slender, poised) has spread its venom,

unseated restraint. Eve thought she could handle
all the knowing, keep its desire in check. So did I,

engaging the shul-boys—and men—in argument, peppery
debate ornate with analogy, each point honed as a needle

darning the fabric of law, material rent and sewn so often
that the body is all seams, meetings where text is tested

against the law's undroppable stitch. I have been tested
and not held up so well. My husband, Rabbi Meir, convinced

of women's mercurial nature, sent a student to seduce me,
proving I carry my gender's flaw. I could have saved him

the trouble. I saw the boy and bisected myself: body
and *shechinah*, material and spirit; I left the good girl

in the kitchen kneading, and searched for stories
to serve—poor substitutions, I know—as explanation.

II.

My mother taught me how to tell a person what he
can hear: in verse, song, parable, anecdote, riddle,

and I often told my husband stories to coax him
toward conclusions. My sons both died on a Sabbath,

53

and I couldn't tell him, couldn't let death infect the day
of rest. He asked, *Where are my sons?* and I turned our loss

into query: *A stranger lent me valuables and wants them back.*
Must I return them? Of course, my husband affirmed, and I

showed him: *The Lord giveth, the Lord...*you know the rest.
My sons, my sons...I felt myself drowning in *halachah*,

our laws, and dreamed myself awash in text, imprinted
on hands and mouth, bracelets of letters, interpretive limbs,

questions covering breasts and back...When the boy
appeared at my door, I tore myself from the page, tearing

the page itself, curious how it would feel to err by intent.
I am cursed with awareness: we favor the simple son

over the wicked; ignorance pales in the flushed light
of conscious decision. Did I boast myself immune to sin?

III.

I should know what lurks behind songs of seduction,
a script's facade—Jews build furnished rooms of meaning

into our words—still so light they can be carried on
our backs, no need (yes desire!) for a temple to house

our scrolls. As I took the boy into my hands, so will I
embrace my own punishment: lithe from the rope's grip,

cleansed of choice. Will I be a symbol for what fails
when a woman—a scholar—purges dust from the texts?

I told my husband to pray for the death of a sin,
not the death of a sinner. Will he pray for me, for my pride,

or for his own soul, that which drove him to act as God
commanding the angel to wrestle Jacob, testing his strength?

Had Jacob failed, would the angel have sung hosannas,
or skulked back to God? And God, in His house on high—

whose side was He on? No punishment fits its crime. One apple:
expulsion, pain, the constant ledge of extinction. I say to Eve:

let sin dissolve into the valence of day and dusk;
let night's calming conscience still the sinner of flux.

Leah and the Mirror-Ball

Rachel says—*you got a friend for my sister?*

They always do, or find one—whatever it takes to get her
into their tight circumference and I watch her laughing
at their weak lines, black hair heightening her features'
harmonious arrangement on the page of her rose-peach

skin. She holds their attention on her tongue like the wine
our father swigs at dinner, hatching pyramid schemes.
Someone has moved the stone from the prolific well
of his mouth; his speeches drown our ears.

Our high school gym disguised as a cavernous beach:
sand in our shoes' grottos, grains down our shirts.
While she's busy projecting her image onto their eyes'
curved screens, I dissipate, pace the porous walls,

brush up against the mingling demons who whisper
you could have him all to yourself, you could be the fairest
and I say *go to hell* and spill spiked punch on their
strange shoes, flash my compact at the mirror-ball

to blind them. She can't go without me—our father's rule.
In learning how to hate him, our wants have merged.
Still, talents diverge: Rachel has beauty, and whatever lies
beneath it. My looks go unmentioned, only that my eyes

"were weak," which I read as reflexive: the one who can't
see must not be worth looking at. Instead, I see what
she can't: tomorrows dip their inks in eyes' sleeping wells.
Rachel shields her ears formed finely as china figurines,

I don't want to know what I can't change. I want to know
what I can change. Then, change. She wants to be a mother?
I'll beat her to it: six boys, one lovely girl who will captivate
a foreign prince. I let the local boy slip inside my shirt:

my tongue is still at these times when talk would inhibit
the will and wandering Rachel refuses. I can't afford to deny
one pleasure—that's her luxury, knowing there'll always be
another. I know when to close my eyes to pity, close for lust,

close for knowing: I can make out a stranger approaching,
one with a walk we'll both like. He'll not expect her to plumb
her own cool sources; her form, he thinks, mirrors her content,
and I wouldn't submit otherwise. He promises to work

seven years for her hand, then claiming *it passed like a week*
as he gazes at the veil disguising me and my deception
as the object of desire. And when morning unfurls his eyelids
once he's covered every circle and square of "her" imaginary

body he'll find me and say *What's this?* My father will smirk
What's another week? while Rachel steeps in anger and I slump,
ashamed of my complicity, still absorbing the skim and press
of his fingers. Seven more years I'll beget tribal names that filter

into the world's backseats. For now, the mirror-ball pricks
the room with light, and stars splatter on our faces, bury
in our skirts. Rachel's arms drape wider shoulders,
today's boy cups the arc of her hip, the band plays love

forlorn. The girls who dance with corner-shadows stack
cookies on plates, then let them fall into patterns we read
as closely as we learn to read faces and bodies—do people
know how much they give away in gesture, in the slip

between expressions? Even from this distance I can see
he'll want her. He'll get me first. *It's not fair*, she'll cry,
and I'll want to laugh like Sarah: with joy, incredulity.
Instead, I'll fold her into the oval of my arms and let her weep.

Isn't He just? Doesn't He evenly distribute His gifts?
(*And the Lord saw that Leah was hated, and he opened
her womb*) She's never questioned what's fair—
and who am I to tell her, who am I to know?

III.

Their words are specks. All the Jews are in the air.
—Cynthia Ozick

Vox Humana

...But the Lord was not in the wind; and after the wind an earthquake;
but the Lord was not in the earthquake; and after the earthquake a fire;
but the Lord was not in the fire; and after the fire a still small voice.

First Kings 19:7

I. Sibilant

A term of limited ambition:
> *having, containing, producing*
> *s or sh in sash.*
> *Sibilare's present participle:*
> *to hiss or whistle.*

Sash:
> *band worn about the waist or over*
> *one shoulder as a dress accessory*
>> —pageant contestants, parading Kiwanis—
>
> *framework in which panes of glass*
> *are set in a window or door*
>> —open space where sounds slip in
>> sift through and settle—

(not in the wind
not in the earthquake
not in the fire)

                batter falling   into the floured pan
                       Vaughan Williams' oboe concerto

     wet   traffic

                    rake making grooves in manicured dirt
    steps' susurrus

                      sigh en route to silence.

II. Complaint

Dead, he looked himself, except
the lips: too thin, too pale, pressed shut,
an expression foreign to his face.
I left the room where he lay, dressed up.

Then went back in. And went back in.
I couldn't get over his lips, so stingily
shaped. I told my somber friends.
Responding, their own lips stiffened.

At a loss for actuality, children proffer
invisible bits of play: mock tea in faux Spode,
fake villainy. At a loss, adults offer less.
Then again, what could they say? *Oh.*

The ease of exhalation. *Oh.* That's how
they released the air they trapped, stalled,
compressed against its will. I don't
blame them. I don't blame them at all

for pairing one absence with another.
Just as well I didn't know that his lips
were sewn shut. A practical matter,
shutting up the dead with stitch—

as if they could protest or quiet
our cries with a tapering *shhhh*, take back
their—decision? They leave us. They leave us
speechless. Our lips grown slack.

III. Chance Music

Tears of dirt tap the carved casket.
Jays' patter, inadequate phrases. Leaves
twist in grief. Cars hiss as they flatten
fresh blacktop on streets that bind
the graveyard into the city's striations.
You know the words, what must be said
to calm the wise, the wicked, the simple,
and he who doesn't know how to ask
the question. You know the tune—it sifts
through lungs, knees, fingertips *largo*
largo scattering winsome riffs.

The poet: *Every tribe has its music.*
The composer: *I prefer inconsistency.*
Your prayer, which I can't understand
or pronounce, sounds like the pouring
of honey into a steaming glass of tea.
Mine sounds like blame, pebbles under
my tongue, an upright bass descending
a sullen scale. The dead has shut his doors,
but our breath still sluices, entreating
the lips to part, to purse, to plea. There is—
there is no heavenly choir. Sing Now.

IV. Threnody

A chirr, a sigh, a minor seventh
        chord—what is grief's natural noise?
        Or does a suit of silence fit
        its form? *Shhhh*—I hear a voice—

its origin—below? above?
        inside the attic of the stones?
        the tree is silent—rings and bark
        except with branches overgrown

        attended by the saw's low purr—
        (chance music in the graveyard's hum)
        so many dead—that's all the music
                they can make? "a formal feeling comes"

        comments E.D.—I add her voice
        to those who use my brain as phone,
        as street to pace—the crowds—I need
        an hour—no less, no, more—alone

                What do I know—of silence, can you
                        tell me how it sounds?   It tastes
                too rich, too dense, surrounds the tongue
                        I want my lips to make its shape—

                like his?—not now, not yet, I can't
                        forgive, I can forget—it needs
                to be the other way around
                    —remember and concede—

            my feet implore this ground inured
                     to pleas—the thrushes waste
                  their song—

no, not a waste, the concerts free
                my vision ebbs—*the lips are wrong*

You and Them

When a guy calls your jazz show
at 2 a.m. and asks for "Kiss Kiss Kiss"
by Yoko Ono, lock the doors.
You're there for two more hours,
and your home Studio A is
the best-lit room for miles
of sleeping suburbs. Studio B
looks like a space-ship,
all knobs, buttons, consoles
and their eerie green lights
that signal go, keep going,
one looks like your heartbeat,
scraggly neon cliffs that repeat
at your pulse's even meter.
A vat of black coffee,
a leaning stack of vinyl,
your microphone, suspended
from a robot's metal arm,
and big, padded earphones
cradling your head.
"It's 2:15 a.m.," you tell
your listeners, reading them
a lullaby of names off the back
of an album. You tell them
a story, the last time you went to
the Blue Note, on your birthday,
Carmen McCrae's 11:30 show.
You held your goblet's stem,
it was glistening and thin,
the barest glass skin around
dark red wine. Your date's
hand alit at the small

of your back. You don't
tell them that, that
would bring the crazies out,
the other insomniacs who want
to be wooed, already so
lonely and a sigh would make them
think you understood. Your voice
has sunk to its lowest pitch,
cadences that barely rise and fall,
you can picture undulations
in the air around your mouth,
they take you farther and farther
out into the darkness where
this sound that represents you
doesn't need you at all.

Dedication

I.

This goes out, as the disc jockeys like to say,
to Alfred—not his real name, not even close.
In fact, appropriately far, so if he chooses
to turn a deaf ear, he can do so. Alfred wrote

one strong novel that debuted to reviews
not quite as smart as he, then disappeared—
Al and his novel, his deco affection, beveled
ego and unfettered questions—to Germany,

perhaps a strange place for a young Jew
with talent these days, but Al is strange,
he thrives on bitter tastes. He told me,
"Manhattan tapers," which, of course,

it does, though I can't recall why he felt
the need to tell me—I'm sure it was part
of some elaborate allusion, my old friend
prone to opacity, though it may have been

a simple response to the question of why
so few bus routes continue south of Houston
when they are increasingly needed—as though
the borough suffers from poor circulation,

narrowing land barren, extremities lacking life-
blood. One never knows. Al has acquired the habit
of knowledge, and sprays it liberally as floral
perfume at a Sweet 16—though it is less cloying.

II.

Alfred, I would like you to consider
coming home. I know that Germany is more

than an attic, but most of my scenes when
I played Anne Frank in high school drama

took place on the gym's drab proscenium stage
dressed down to resemble the Secret Annexe,
and each time I said, "I still believe that people
are really good at heart," I believed it less;

"I think that it will all come right" made me
downright depressed, even acting as poorly as I do—
cast to type, a young Jewess, my asset that I could
cry on command, though Anne rarely cries,

and I did all the time. We used lamps
that dissembled as candles, and looked like
candles cloaked in glass, and one night,
convinced that they were candles, I knew

with a certainty rare at the time: one false move
would burn down the house. Pinocchio under
my skin—convinced that with effort, one could
transform the wooden self, change artifice

to the authentic, lamp to wick and wax and flame,
the tip reaching up to lick my face and the face
of the boy cast as Peter, my maybe-lover in hiding.
I prayed for reinvention, my own transubstantiation.

III.

Pretending our characters' lines did not augur
their deaths, pretending that we did not know
we would die—we, the late and lucky, religious-
schooled in guilt, quizzed on concentration camp

names, taught the poems of young martyrs,
our flattened vowels so far a cry from the glottal
sonata of German and Yiddish that I wondered
how the world would know we were Jewish,

whether the midwest had purged the shouting
and wringing of hands from our family dinners—
my tribe remote from the multisyllabics of names
changed at Ellis Island. How would anyone know?

Could you pass? says Alfred's voice, droll in the cave
of my ear. My grandma Rose would say, *The world
won't let you forget*, shaking her prodigious head,
waggling a finger, and while I roll my eyes and make

the mouth of God-rest-her-soul, I don't know
whether to hope that she is wrong or right.
This distrust, distilled: what we carry and sit with,
walk with, lie down and rise up with, wear

on our hands, as a frontlet between our eyes.
This goes out to Alfred, deep in the gutteral
throat of a language, the curious love of return
that ferries him over dark water, with gifts.

Through the Blinds

Every night he comes back and I nudge you, "There. There."
like a child convinced of her reappearing monster, and you

who would awaken to kiss the tips of my fingers if I asked,
don't budge. I point past you out the two-pane window.

This is no monster. This is my great-grandfather, also a tree,
lifting his arms toward heaven in a futile shrug, as if to say

"Why?"or "Why not?" He is gaunt. He reminds me
that where I am I may as well be, here is a fine place to root,

to marry a man who would shake himself from sleep
to see me pleased but for some reason can't see this man-tree

from Minsk or Pinsk, we don't know—I must be the one
to see things, to pluck him from lore, from rhyme,

the dull roar of family history—*a general*, my mother says,
in the Russian army. We are in a new state, with names

that ask the tongue and teeth to perform salacious tricks
on language, curlings and clicks—not the gargle and spit

of Yiddish, tone of rue, *I'll believe it when I see it*
though we pray to a God we can't see, we implore,

a sighting—yet we have no one to sight. I have someone!
I shout in my sleep. A eucalyptus—tall Joseph, carpenter

born nobleman—how else would he show himself but steeped
in wood, thinly barked? He pulls his sky down to eye-level,

traps a moon in his gesture. Or does he hold up the firmament,
a lone pole, bowing—cantilever seeking its mate? I ask,

what do you want to be? willing to cast another line

for his purpose here, willing to recast history, if need be.

The street is silent save a lisp leftover from the ocean's day—
and it is his humming, too. A sweet Russian 12-bar blues.

Myths of Travel

"Should we have stayed at home, wherever that may be?"
—E. Bishop

Sanguine sugar maples like tubes of red lipstick line
the dotted-line road from Mt. Blue to Skowhegan.
We're lost, he tells her. *We are lost, we are lost*
repeat the wheels in somersault, taking on pebbles
like a lifeboat sprung a negligible (is there such an animal?) leak.

"Find us," he says, and hands her the map, the legend
that matches symbol to distance, destination—
synecdoche at work, scaling down the sine wave
of mountain and table to a mottled crosshatch in gray, in pink,
water always green or blue or both, the shape of a river

whose boundaries elude the level eye, made explicit.
She traces the interstate's offshoots, lanes once Main Streets,
notes towns with worldly or declamatory names
like Paris and Freedom. Who wouldn't live in Paris, in Freedom?
She says, "it's an adventure" and "just over the next big hill"—

which do not make him laugh, and she realizes
how much she hates the myths of travel—that it's "broadening,"
that at trip's inexorable end, you're ready to go home.
She tells him where to turn and he does so, slowly,
suspicious of her restless ziggurat, craving one straight line

between X and Y, unlike her route—akin, he claims
to Moses' serpentine trek. He's tired of craning
his neck at mundanities: crowds of standing cows—she says
"they bode fair weather"—bloated farms with mud-red shingles,
the overgrown geometry of baseball fields with rusted backstops.

The legend (like all good stories) points them home.
Must home be an end? The trip a symbol? Cartographic

(half an inch, 20 miles) or enlarged so that they look back
with hindsight's vague powers of analysis: *the cow meant something;
the barn, something; the backstop, definitely something...*

Sure that they have circled the statue of an ersatz Davy Crockett
ten times—she says, "each town has its own"—he asks directions
of a skeptic who drawls in the Mainer's patient speech,
"You can't get there from here"—a phrase that in all
its dubious ambiguity, sounds more cryptic than it is.

Song of Hearing

How is it that I want your voice to sound?
A mirror or a mimic of my own
exaggerated duly by the phone,
the way a mime would follow me around?
And could you imitate my pitch and tone—
lift up your voice when mine does, let it down
when mine declines—the cord between us wound
so penitently tight, I hear it moan?

Imagine we were children, singing rounds,
each melody repeated till it's honed,
and on one fabled afternoon you found
your voice resembled mine, as if I'd thrown
my words into your mouth, my verbs and nouns,
to lodge beneath your tongue, like teaching-stones.
You spit my language out onto the ground
and since then, what we hear, we hear alone.

New York Water

I heard that New York water stinks.
An ex-New Yorker told me so
implying that she ought to know.
I'm loathe to tell her that I think

she's wrong, that New York water tastes
as smooth as scotch that's old and rare,
as clean as ocean-scented air.
In fact, I would not want to waste

a single drop on her complaints.
Thank God she left. We do not need
ungrateful whiners, bad seeds, weeds
among us. She should buy a Saint

Bernard and go to Switzerland
to yodel in the Alpish air
and drink their water, if she dares
to buy a bottle, at a grand

expense. It's fine for millionaires.
I trust these pipes, their flakes, their lead.
I doubt that you will find me dead
from poison liquids, pens, or stares.

Admittedly, there's much to fear
from city life—the rat, the roach,
the roach-like realtor who'd encroach
upon your dreams, the cabbie's leer,

construction beams that rest above
your waiting head, the crowds, the crime—
and yet there's much that is sublime.
And that includes the water, love.

Bats in Maine

You call to tell about the bats,
the way they course and crease the air
beneath the rafters where they wait
for night, above the attic stairs.

I envy them. I envy them
their flights above your midnight bed,
the pacing figure eights they wend
to find an out, in certain dread

of being trapped inside a place
too small to dive or weave or swoop,
too small to make their pattern lace
two side-walls in a sightless loop.

You do not dream of me, I know.
I do not dream at all, you say.
Your memories of me come and go
but unlike bats, won't go away

completely through the broken pane
you claim you want to fix and heal,
that fracture that you choose to feign
forgotten, that you would conceal.

I wish I had those eerie eyes
that see and can be seen their best
at nighttime, when we best disguise
the wingspan of our deep unrest.

Song of Disparity

I would have liked to sing but was not tapped
        for the voice—
one per village, per island, per borough, burg, villa.

You, they wanted. Were they among the throng
        outside the audition room,
lissome tails hidden under long peasant skirts

we wore with leotards and boots, to accentuate
        the fluted waist,
long line, fathom of our breaths, hoisting the blue

and bright notes up a cord that splays, plays out in
        the throat and cave
of the mouth? Your songs: one from "Patience,"

the wistful title tune from "Anyone Can Whistle"
        and one Mermanesque,
"Don't Rain on My Parade," made famous

by another ballsy Jew, picked to demonstrate
        your range, your gifts
for patter, ballad, belt. I could not connect

the sonority that swept through the ribcage
        of an old Broadway building,
under the door marked Do Not Disturb

with the black-haired ingenue in t-strapped
        character shoes,
with the girl who sang mezzo to my mundane alto,

my voice the axis to your sine wave, round tones
        that spoke to a wider world
while I hit perfunctory notes on key. That much

I could do. An occasional hint of vibrato, a veer
                    toward some pure scheme,
but mostly I left that to you. Who will sing

the pretty parts, the agile scales, now that the sirens
                    have stolen you,
partial, particle from the burning ship? Lifeboats

brimming with those who stayed up top, prolonging
                    their wishes
on the North Sea's riot of stars. Must I take on

the role of Callas-widow, and weep beneath
                    your tendriled balcony,
your midtown fire escape, vowing that I will

never truly hear another? I don't understand how
                    fire survives in water
that eventually will quash flame's will, but I know

how a voice can settle itself upon another's shoulders
                    like a coat lent
for warmth. And the coat becomes heavy, gift shifts

to burden. Who has ever loved equally, Ruth?
                    When your biblical namesake
clung to Naomi's scant material, *entreat me not*

to leave thee, did the elder's heart swell
                    with adoration—or pity?
The letter of the law is wrong: what's fair

is not fair. We all want parity, and though I
                    did not send you away,
I did not say, *stay. Let me be a friend.*

You and your voice left to woo frigid air
                    with show tunes, duets,
plotting a course along currents that feed

the perfectly pitched ears of those versed in
                    formless serenade—
who would dare to sing to them? One with nothing

to lose, as flame's tongue lingers over
                              what it consumes.
They wove through you, sifting will

from instinct, lyric from lyrics sewn in your tongue
            like labels affixed
to collars of childhood. They will teach you

new ways to breath and phrase, though as to why
                    you sing—
that won't change—lure and allure still the thing.

Is that you at the door? I thought that I heard
                    a refrain,
a coda from the vacant cove, the awning

where strangers wait out the rain at the invitation
            of emptiness.
In a quiver that dissolves and rises up again,

in the concave lull between city squall
                    and calm,
in the wake that follows a crowd's trawl

up and down the avenues, threading streets
                          numbered off,
accounted for—in finale, where chorus girls quietly

surrender the illusion of sameness, and each sings
            only the line
that her voice dictates, abandoning balance and blend

to backstage, darkening wings—I hear you, Ruth,
                    your speechless name:
convert to rune, to threnody.

You Should Know By Now

that Wednesday cars (those that hit the assembly line midweek,
Monday's, Tuesday's hangovers subsided, before bleak Thursday,
Friday's paycheck) were nothing but Detroit folklore—but you love
the idea of the ideal, of fate and fury conspiring, and there was a way
to pick a Wednesday car, a marking, if you knew where to look.

No one ever did,

says your brother who spent his teenage summers at camp
on the line—River Rouge, Zug Island. You never worked like that,
no one wanted you to sweat on shifts, your job to outsmart
the nay-saying doctors, your mother 40 at your birth. When you
had the right amount of fingers and toes, they rejoiced.

Child of doubt,

you subscribe to belief, less in the God of love or justice
than in vagaries of myth, local (between four less than exemplary
days of work lies one of precision, a locus of perfection)
and ancient (Odysseus, bound to his ship, craved a song
of experience, straining his bonds to join its origin).

You want to hear,

so you sacrifice fact at the altar of story, drawn to your father's
fables of his five older brothers, Toronto boys in downtown Detroit
who could outdrink anyone—on whiskey or gin. On beer they were
sunk, Canadian rubes, all dead now, long before your father died,
before you were forced to forgive his flawed heart for expiring.

You should know by now,

ghosts are fictions—but when you last saw his vague shape
he looked well, a bit thin. *Buy yourself a Wednesday car,* he said.
You said, *I can't tell one—is the marking on the fender?* And he grinned.

You pay lip service to denial, but there he was: two whole legs
instead of the halves he was left with, the ghost pain.

You love your fictions,

must not confess your suspicions that he lives beneath your eyelid,
in the echo your ear's factory won't release. Must our senses
be entrusted with truth? You fear losing your faith in his timbre,
growing deaf to a song that lures you to where he is whole.
Don't forget: the doubt that carried you into this world

could drive him away.

lower case (ii)

Storm the castle, he says.
I am playing a board game
with god. We each own property
with several green homes, red hotels.
He gives me bad advice so I will lose.
Not on your life, I say.

His turns take awhile.
Decisions are not his forte.
The clock is ticking, I say.
Then I tick like a clock,
move my arms like hands.
I wish you'd stop, he mutters.

I raise my eyebrows. *Temper, temper.*
Then I stop. He stares
at the plastic tokens as though
the cardboard city will drown them
in its stiff bisection, as though
their suede pouch is eternity

and the right move will save them.
I happen to be good at this, taught
to buy everything: spend, spend
and waste no time in jail. Luck, however,
eludes me. I look up to find him
glaring a hole in Park Place

and there, my strategy crumbles.
He wins, strong in the clutch,
with a gift for rolling doubles.
Just as well: I'm a better loser.
Again? he says. I shake my head.
We share one beer and fold things up.

Pythagoras, Undone

Give credit where histories eddy: Egyptians stretched a cord,
    formed a triangle, sides of 3, 4, and 5, and found 90 degrees
        between the two short legs. Later, Pythagoras declared

that given an angle called "right," anyone capable of squaring
    two sides could find the third. He and the brotherhood believed
        that the Lord provided rational numbers, so when pi was proven

to bleed ad continuum, nauseam, into the night, fraternity
    waned. Rumor has it that townies, scorning the math crowd's
        aristocratic days spent in theory, enacted a massacre—the
                              masses

tired of being told, *the world makes sense, numbers possess*
    colors and virtues. Others say the old man died of broken spirit,
        the school dissolving, his two sons at odds, at sixes and sevens.

                         *   *   *

The math teacher on the plane who turned toward me when we
    hit our bumpy stride between layers of fluff presented this as
        a good story, one that allowed him, who wondered why

his students' love of numbers was null, to introduce a man
    into the equation. Staring out at no horizon but a murky cusp,
        he crosshatched his fingers and settled his voice into the long,
                              long

ago mode, already pleased, admiring a figure who could die
    of broken faith in a God who made numbers complex as man,
        pure numbers dissembling as order now bleary-eyed, endless.

                         *   *   *

And worse: God giving the irrational such ignoble trappings,
    a runt that couldn't reach 3.2, the old man's greatest fears
        realized—how would we know, now, what answers lie within

our purview? Or would we seek the easy out when limits
    turned coy? Pythagoras could take no comfort from love
        of infinity, having believed that the overturned eight

was God's franchise, reserved for the span of sky beyond
    where the eye could draw image. And now to find it common,
        confined within all circles, a wheel attached to no vehicle,

a coin of no value—history a litany of letdowns, delayed
    only by the years between men who distractedly drew lines
        in sand, wanting and dreading what they couldn't know.

*   *   *

I imagine our plane banked by scrims depicting fat clouds,
    a slim strip of sunset, murals unrolling like parchment
        as we fly through, aloof to artifice—and am grateful

that surrounding us on all four sides are air and water, that we
    can breach this infinity and leave it in peace—I have less stake
        in the rational than the old Greek, who took his solace there.

Perhaps he won my friend's heart by devotion, not to lover or land,
    but to theorem, a retinue of theory—and what in return? A squared
        hypotenuse, the sum of two squared sides, and one perfectly
                              right angle.

Persuasion

In the evening, an animated salesman, a cartoon version of a man,
    Mel Farr, flew into the firmament,
           leisure suit topped by a cape, a vast, gold "M"
across his chest, prepared to offer deals on the full line of Fords and
                                           Lincolns,
      prices slashed like evil
        in my wayward metropolis, Detroit.

I waited for my mother's footsteps as Mel Farr soared and promoted
    his wares. A boy's deft hand
        found the clasp of my bra and dismissed it
with a flick. He whispered, "my dad and Mel Farr are 'like this'"
    marrying two fingers, that hand
        distraction, the other wandering in nervous circles.

His desire and mine, curiosity, my father's metronomic snoring—
    that's what it takes: balance
        of elements and humours, all good planets
in line, Mel Farr in the stratosphere—unwitting cupid, his salespitch
    background music to a static
        seduction. I imagined Mel in the showroom,

navigating straits between cars named for horses and mythical heroes,
    foreign words for speed, light, and wind,
        then flying into a sky-blue backdrop, his telegenic
image indelible, spondaic name impressed upon that night's
    constellation. The boy's name
        has dimmed, replaced by clusters of memory

dense as inky nights flush with stars, far from that city, any city,
    far from intervening light.
        I let him think that he could talk his way
in and under, the way a good salesman can—perhaps now
    he would rather be known
        for some other talent, but then, that was enough.

Inventory

I ate my lunch next to Rocky, the shy man
who showed me which parts to count.
His wife and young son brought his lunch
every day. We smiled and talk about
Twelve Oaks Mall, and I was embarrassed
to be such a college girl. But, Rocky told me,
you're a good worker. He saved me from John,
a huge blond guy who "majored in football"
at some Texas school. *I never went out*
with a high-class girl from Farmington Hills,
he said, and I told him, *I grew up in Detroit*
and I have a steady boyfriend, which were true
and John said, *I could take him,* which was
also true. Rocky told John to leave me alone,
and sometimes he did and sometimes he'd
follow me down Novi Road for a couple of miles
before turning off. I drove a tin can with no
pickup, and kept John in my right-hand
mirror—the one that makes everything
farther away—and pretended to sing with the radio,
counting beats between bumps in the road.

Three Layers

Smack in the middle of Elton John's "Honky Chateau,"
    streaks of syncopated chords that shoot
        from the fingers in apparent spontaneity,
            a head-sized chunk of metal

smacked a windshield like a mythical bat's homerun,
    creating a dent in its own image,
        the dash and seat of the passenger side
            spattered in glass sparks, the shield

a spiderweb of spun threads. The car ahead made
    the metal a projectile, striking
        at such an angle that it rose
            from the pocked road into the chaos of air,

posing a problem made of words: if X and Y travel toward
    each other at speed too fast,
        the distance between them too short,
            how long until they meet?

No way to solve for T, no time to swerve as shards
    dressed and peppered
        the body missing from the passenger seat.
            Praise safety glass! Three patented layers:

the first absorbs impact, the middle gives glue,
    the third denies the impulse
        to break into jaggedness,
            reducing itself to fractions

smattered like paint from Pollack's wild wrist and tools.
    And praise the hollow lack of company,
        fate's penchant for filling up voids
            matched only by its will to excite

the benign from inertia. How much force did X need
    to prevail, to carve its shape
        into the glass curve, the unmarred arc
            demanding a flaw—human error insufficient?

II.

I've seen the reverse: a windshield after a head pushed it out,
    the fist at the end of a torso
        swinging forward like a hammer,
            demanding exit. En route home, I shrank

from the neon cones lining the shoulder, some supine. I shrank
    from the brown bag that floated up,
        diverted by a trickster wind—
            the highway an obstacle course

of equal or greater competing forces in disguise. The night before
    we talked of the overpass,
        the railroad tie pushed over,
            the man who died, as the metal propelled

by boys and gravity poured through the car's steel ceiling.
    Descent outdoes ascent,
        and I will give him that, the franchise
            on tragedy, though as children we fought

over who was worse off, tested ourselves against pain.
    I am over wondering
        what I can handle—drama shows up
            in droves, unannounced—I have plenty

without inviting more. I am not willing to say that my mind
    was elsewhere, that I lose myself
        in the scaffolding tower whose lights
            sputter squib-like, luring planes from smog,

or that I scrutinize signs that offer deals and lovelife advice.
    I was as conscious as I've ever been,
        which has sufficed. Consider one
           of the three great washes of feeling:

a car, a radio, a seamless day, a DJ spinning a song you've stored
    with your name. And you heard
        your own voice's off-key clarion.
          So little to protect us from impulse,

love of crucible. How eagerly we flew to meet.

Consolation

I am the person going over Victoria Falls
        in a rowboat, in a children's pop-up book.
When she opens to my page, the cascades
        project and my small craft teeters just over
the edge. Each time her face shows surprise
        that the rapids haven't pushed me down
farther—she thinks that I, like her, comprise
        beginning, middle, end—when, in fact, I am
suspended, atop a splatter of mist and spray.
        My hands with their undenoted fingers
clutch the boat's lip. My face, a slight smear
        of features, the gesture of a fine-point pen—
gives nothing away. But I am not scared—
        why should I fear what the natives call,
"smoke that thunders," the drop I'll repeat
        until paper or mechanism wear, until
her focus strays? Book closed, I am flat
        with the falls, a slice of the Zambezi.
I can't complain. I know that the brightest star
        is Sirius, the dog star, nine short light-years
from this fold, my plight. And in these
        long nights, as my appeal wanes, I dry off
and do my best to find it.

On Forgettings

I.

Consider the view from my bedroom window: a graveyard
brimming with Houston's oldest Jews to pass in this swelter.
Their land overlooks, filters into the bayou, adrift toward
the Gulf that submits to the ocean's tow, or gives itself away.

I took to them, invited them in across the sinuous road
where bikers dragged their grooves into the asphalt,
oblivious to the dead or living yearning for quiet.
What do I know of silence? The quiet in their wake

is worse—the harbinger of noise, and waiting is an ache
not local but broad, a hapless messenger who takes his share
of heat—we say *the wait is worse* but I say *it prepares us.*
I say *we fall in love with it and blame it for leaving.*

II.

Down West Dallas Ave. lies a freedmens' graveyard,
notched in the city street's dubious progress, stones
hardly visible, weed-doused, cloaked in a raucous tangle,
fist-sized insects and snakes driven from the Ireland

of cultivated parks. And though I wonder why no one
cleans these slate faces, why wildflowers scrawl their lines
over epitaphs, I know my indignation exists to stave off
the scarcity that I will become, the sum of name and date.

Perhaps weeds shade the sheer stones from harsh light,
save the denizens from scrutiny, vines connecting gravesites
as though beneath, the deads' hands touch: death no divorce
from yearning. We say *the wait is worse,* as though it ends.

III.

My father's cemetery planted squarely in Detroit
where Woodward Ave. elbows 8 Mile Road—Machpelah,
named for the cave and field where Abraham rested Sarah,
and after a hundred threescore and fifteen years, found his place.

Ten years passed, this corner still uncrowded: recent dead
lie closer to where their children dwell, in suburb and exurb,
and the migrating young will need directions to trace
their attenuated names. Here, the buried lie discrete, joined

by vowel-less Hebrew, six-pointed stars—and if their hands
touch, we have no sign of it. My father drifts further and farther
into memory, his grave becoming one in a sea of stones, engraved.
We say *the wait is worse* when we mean, the forgetting.

Vertical

Flame doesn't rise above the wax we indented
on one side to provide the melt
an out, so the listing wick won't die in liquid,
though it always does, the woven
string slumps toward its version of earth, hot paraffin—
home, its very own drowning pool.

Two gladiolas near my hand are beanstalks, I'd
climb their arc if not for how you
curve to me in sleep, how the drapes glisten, book spines
glow. I make the fire disappear
between wet fingertips—you don't need ornament,
what scarce light finds you is flattered,

graced by luck, like the boy who trades his mild cow for
magic beans and doesn't get duped.

Concatenate

There is nothing wrong with this night.
There is nothing wrong that I can't reconcile:
frogs' soprano, doves' alto, shed doors straining
against the steel chain that forces them together
when they'd rather go their own ways; dissonance
of heat in the dark; ceiling fan making particles
mingle that would choose to stay separate
if they had the power of choice.

Tonight, I am the animating factor.
Tonight, I am the little god, nominated
by my screen door clicking open-shut-open
in an almost danceable rhythm, of its own
volition—one of the many beneficiaries
of free will, one of the victims.

ABOUT THE AUTHOR

Patty Seyburn grew up in Detroit, and has lived in Chicago, New York, Los Angeles, and Houston. She holds degrees from Northwestern University, and worked as a journalist for seven years before earning her M.F.A. in poetry from the University of California, Irvine. She is currently completing her Ph.D. in literature and creative writing at the University of Houston. She works as a freelance journalist, and teaches composition and poetry in person, and by mail and e-mail. She lives in Southern California with her husband, Eric Little.